TALES OF HORROR

MONSTERS

Jim Pipe

TALES OF HORROR
MONSTERS

Acknowledgements

Copyright © 2006 *ticktock* Entertainment Ltd.

First published in Great Britain by ticktock Media Ltd.,

Unit 2, Orchard Business Centre, North Farm Road, Tunbridge Wells, Kent TN2 3XF, Great Britain.

A CIP catalogue record for this book is available from the British Library.

ISBN 1 84696 017 7 Printed in China.

Picture Credits:

t=top, b=bottom, c=centre, l=left, r=right, OFC=outside front cover, OBC=outside back cover.
Corbis: 18-19 (main pic). Getty: 6cl, 7 (main pic), 16/17 (main pic). Everrett/Rex Features: OFC, 6tl, 26/27. Shutterstock: 1, 12bl, 13tr, 14/15 (main pic),
14tl, 22tl, 24/25 (main pic: lizard), Linda Bucklin 4/5 (main pic), Christian Darkin 28bl, Domhnall Dods 20/21 (main pic), Rudolf Georg 26tl (main pic),
Milos Jokic 24/25 (main pic: chicken), Adrian T Jones 16bl, LEACH 4bl, Emily H Locklear 24bl, Ritu Manoj Jethani 28/29 (main pic), Mark 30tl,
Marina Cano Trueba 30/31. Alex Tomlinson: 8/9 (main pic). ticktock Media image archive: 10/11 (main pic), 10tl, 10bc, 12/13 (main pic),18tl, 21bl, 25bl,
27bl. c. Universal/Everrett/Rex Features: 22/23.

Every effort has been made to trace the copyright holders and we apologize in advance for any unintentional ommissions.

We would be pleased to insert the appropriate acknowledgement in any subsequent edition of this publication.

CONTENTS

WHAT IS A MONSTER?

A great roar echoes around the valley. The ground shakes. Suddenly, a giant shape comes crashing through the trees. Watch out, there's a monster about!

How can you tell if you are looking at a monster? First, look at the size. Most monsters are big. Big enough to swallow you in one bite. Now check out the face. Monsters are ugly, ugly, ugly. Still not sure? Look for huge claws or a mouth full of razor-sharp teeth.

Monsters don't take prisoners. If they don't gobble you up, they'll rip off your head or chew off your arms. Others will toast you with their fiery breath. You have been warned!

If there is a monster living near you, bad luck! Monsters don't die easily. Some have magical powers. If you want to get rid of a monster you'll need to be brave, clever and have superhuman strength!

THE GOOD, THE BAD AND THE UGLY

Don't judge a monster by its looks. Tiny fiends can have evil magical powers. A mighty monster like King Kong can be gentle. An ugly ogre like Shrek can turn out to be a good friend. A beautiful mermaid may lead you to a terrible death.

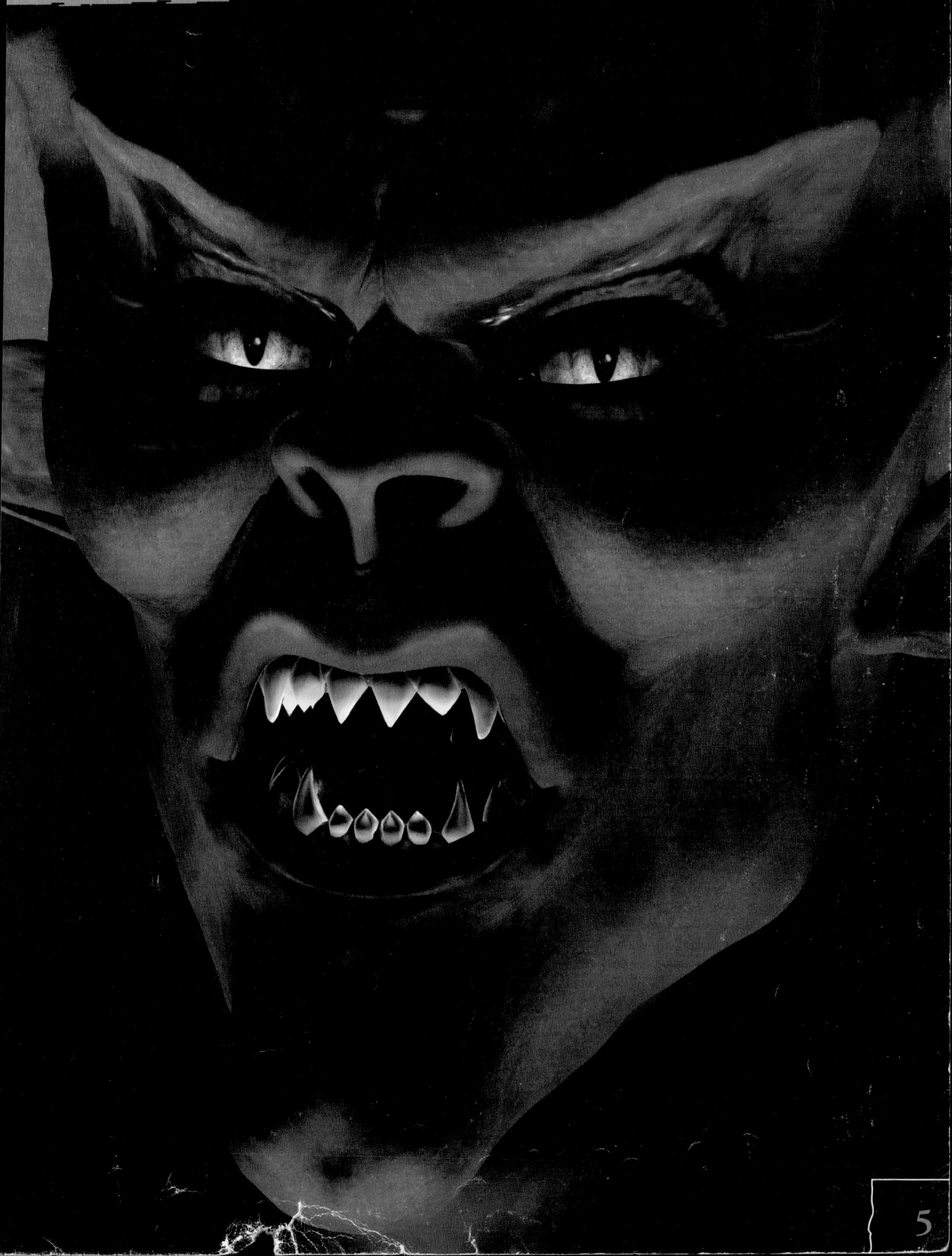

SHY OR SCARY?

Monsters may be nasty and scary, but they can also be shy. Many avoid towns and cities. Where is the best place to find a monster?

Monsters like to hang out in wild, lonely places such as forests, swamps and moors. These are great places for leaping out on people. No one can hear your screams!

Giant, hairy apes have been spotted on mountains across the world. In Asia, this shy creature is known as the Yeti. In North America it is called Bigfoot or Sasquatch. In September 1967, rancher Roger Patterson filmed a tall, shaggy creature in the mountains of northern California. It looked straight at the camera, then vanished into the woods. Was this Bigfoot?

HERE BE MONSTERS!

On 15th century maps, scary monsters marked unexplored waters. Even today, terrible creatures may be hidden deep in our jungles and oceans.

In the story of King Kong, a movie crew land on mysterious Skull Island in the Indian Ocean. They discover a giant ape, packs of killer dinosaurs and swarms of man-eating insects and slugs.

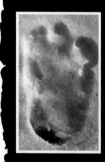

YETI HUNTERS

In September 1951, mountaineer Eric Shipton photographed giant footprints in the snow. Shipton said "where we had to jump crevasses you could see clearly where the creature had dug its toes in." But no Yeti has ever been caught, dead or alive.

MONSTER HUNT

In December 1938, fishermen caught the ugliest fish they had ever seen. It had large, bulging eyes and thick scales. The creature was a coelacanth – a fish that was supposed to have died out 65 million years ago!

Who knows what else is out there? There are still parts of the world where no person has ever been – hidden valleys deep in the jungle, or mountains that can only be reached by helicopter.

Every year, expeditions go in search of monsters like the Yeti or the Loch Ness Monster. Trackers look for unusual marks on the ground. Scientists use hi-tech equipment to search for the creatures underwater or at night.

In 1986, Operation Deepscan used sonar equipment to detect a 73 metre-long shape under the water in Loch Ness, Scotland. Could this be Nessie, the Loch Ness Monster, hiding from the world?

In 2005, an expedition went deep into the Gobi Desert to search for the "Mongolian Death Worm". Locals reported seeing a fat, bright red worm about a metre long. They said it spat out a deadly yellow poison!

GIANTS AND LITTLE PEOPLE

Fee Fi Fo Fum. If you hear these words, run! A giant is on its way. Size isn't everything though. Little people can also make your life difficult!

As well as being huge and very strong, giants can be stupid and mean. Their cousins are ogres and trolls. Like giants, they love the taste of human flesh. Luckily, these big bruisers stay at home a lot – counting their piles of treasure.

In the Middle Ages, some people claimed they had dug up the skulls of a cyclops. This ancient giant had one huge eye in the middle of its forehead. The skulls turned out to be elephant skulls. the "eye socket" was the hole for the elephant's trunk!

A TALL TALE

Giant stories are partly based on famous real-life giants. In the Bible, the future King David kills Goliath. He is a giant warrior, said to be 3 metres tall.

The tallest man in modern times was the American Robert Wadlow. He was 2.7 metres tall when he died in 1940.

LITTLE PEOPLE

All over the world, "little people" are often blamed when things go wrong. These tiny terrors are known as pixies, goblins, fairies, elves or gremlins.

In the Zulu myths of southern Africa, Abatwa are tiny humans. They can ride on ants! Beware, they are armed with deadly poison arrows.

MIXED-UP MONSTERS!

In 2001, news reports from New Delhi, India, told of a vicious beast. Half-man, half-monkey, it was about 1.2 metres tall. It watched its victims with glowing red eyes and attacked them with metal claws.

Some of the scariest monsters are part-human, part-beast. The Sphinx, which appears in Greek myths, had the head of a woman and the body of a lion. It wouldn't let people pass by, until they had answered a question. It strangled anyone who got the answer wrong.

Centaurs also appeared in ancient myths, and more recently Harry Potter. These fierce creatures had the head and chest of a human, and the body of a horse. Their food was raw flesh.

MONSTER FAMILY

Echidna was half woman and half serpent. Her partner was Typhon, a fire-breathing dragon with a hundred heads. Together they made a family of ancient Greek horrors. Among the little darlings were the Chimera, the Hydra, the Sphinx and Cerberus. The worst was probably the Chimera. It was a fire-breathing creature, made up of four different animals.

HUMAN OR MONSTER?

Some monsters can disguise
themselves as humans!
A bloodsucking vampire
can look like you. If you
look closely you will be able
to spot one. Their pointed
fangs are usually a give-away.

FIERCE AND FIERY

"**M**y armour is like tenfold shields, my teeth are swords, my claws spears, the shock of my tail a thunderbolt, my wings a hurricane, and my breath death!"

A dragon! This dragon appears in J.R.R. Tolkein's *The Hobbit* (1937). For hundreds of years, people in Europe lived in fear of dragons. These evil, fire-breathing monsters had the claws of a lion, a spiky tail, scaly skin and wings like a bat. But do they really exist?

Dragons seem to look a lot like snakes and crocodiles. The first dragon stories were probably larger-than-life tales about crocodiles and snakes. The Roman historian Pliny described giant lizards living in India that attacked and killed elephants. These were probably crocodiles. In 450 BC, the Greek writer Herodotus described seeing two dragons in Arabia that had been caught and put in an iron cage. Who knows what they really were...

REAL-LIFE DRAGONS?

In 1912 explorers found a giant lizard on an Indonesian island. It was strangely similar to another well-known monster, the dragon. So, they named it the Komodo dragon.

The Komodo can grow up to 3 metres long. Swift and strong, it has poisonous saliva. It can kill a buffalo three times its size by poisoning it.

Komodo dragons have killed over 25 people in the last 70 years.

SKY MONSTERS

Prometheus lay chained to a rock. In the distance he could see a giant eagle. It was coming to rip out his liver. That night, his liver grew again, ready for the eagle's next visit.

MOTHMAN

In November 1966, five men were digging a grave in West Virginia, USA. Suddenly, something that looked like a "brown human being", with glowing red eyes, flew over them.

Over the next few weeks, there were other sightings of this creature. Some people think it was a Great Horned Owl, shown here. But would you mistake this owl for a human?

This ancient Greek story shows that dragons aren't the only flying terrors. Some of the most deadly monsters attack down from the sky. They snatch up victims in their claws and carry them away.

Harpies are winged monsters with faces like old women. They have long hair and claws made of brass. They punish people who anger the gods by stealing their food. However, anything a harpy touches instantly rots, so harpies always look thin and hungry.

MONSTERS OF THE DEEP

For hundreds of years, sailors have reported attacks by giant squids, slippery sea serpents and other dark monsters. Do they really exist?

"I just saw this grey mass and thrashing tail fin... I didn't see the shark coming as it attacked from underneath. I suddenly felt this enormous pressure, like being gripped in a vice. It wrapped its teeth around the board and my hip, and lifted me out of the water."

An attack by a 3 metre-long Great White Shark, in April 2004, near Port Elizabeth, South Africa. Remember that shark attacks are rare. In fact, falling coconuts kill 15 times more people each year than sharks!

In the 18th century, Dutch captain Jean Magnus Dens was sailing off the coast of West Africa. Two vast arms rose out of the waves. They snatched two of his crew and dragged them under the water. Few believed his story. Then, in the 1940s, a giant squid was measured at 53 metres long!

Few places are as mysterious as the deep ocean. In places it is almost 10 kilometres deep. However, scientists are beginning to explore these cold, dark waters. They use small underwater craft known as submersibles.

In 2002, a mysterious sound, like a giant beast lurking in the ocean depths, was recorded. In March 2006, an eyeless crab-like animal covered in silky blond fur was discovered in the South Pacific. It was over 2 kilometres below the surface.

COULD YOU BECOME A MONSTER?

FROM HUMAN TO MONSTER

Some monsters are born ugly. Others are victims of evil spells or curses. Be careful about who you annoy. You could be next!

In ancient China, people believed their relatives sometimes turned into flesh-eating monsters called Taotie after they died. Taotie had horns and fangs and were half bull, half tiger.

In the Middle Ages, people believed witches could turn themselves into werewolves or vampires. Anyone suspected of being a witch was put on trial. Thousands of innocent people were found guilty and burnt to death.

Many comic book characters are humans with the power to turn into monsters. Spiderman's enemy the "Lizard" is scientist Curt Connors. After taking a powerful drug, Connors grows into a two-legged reptile. He has tough scales like an alligator, wickedly sharp teeth and claws and the powerful tail of a crocodile.

A BAD HAIR DAY

In Greek myths, if you made the gods angry, you were
in trouble! Medusa's mother made a big mistake when she
said her daughter looked prettier than the goddess Athena.
Athena changed Medusa's hair into snakes and her teeth
into tusks. Medusa's tongue turned black and became too large
for her mouth, and her hands became bronze claws.
If anyone looked at Medusa, they turned into stone.

GENE POWER

Scientists have the power to create new kinds of animals. In the 1990s they created a "geep", a half-sheep, half-goat mix.

Other scientists have injected mice with jellyfish genes, making them glow bright green.

Not everyone agrees with these experiments. But the new science may help scientists to make new medicines or grow disease-resistant crops.

SCIENCE MONSTERS

The scene: a mad scientist's lab. A huge corpse lies on a slab. Lightning leaps from across the room. It sends a jolt of electricity through the still body. Underneath the sheet, something twitches. The monster is alive!

Monsters can be made when science experiments go wrong. In Mary Shelley's *Frankenstein* (1818), a scientist sews together a monster using parts from dead bodies he has stolen. Then he uses electricity to breath life into the creature.

In R.L. Stevenson's *The Strange Case of Dr. Jekyll and Mr. Hyde* (1886), scientist Dr Jekyll drinks a powerful drug. He turns into Mr Hyde, a monstrous killer.

In *The Hulk* (2003), radiation poisoning turns scientist Bruce Banner into an ugly green giant when he gets angry. Not even the army can stop him when he turns into the Hulk. In the movie *The Fly* (1958), a scientist mixes his genes with those from a fly. He becomes a half-man, half-fly. Like a real fly, he has to be sick over his food before he can eat it!

MONSTER TALES

Over the years, writers have dreamed up all sorts of monsters. If you believe them, blood-sucking vampires, mutants, killer robots and aliens have walked amongst us.

Some of the stranger ones were written about in the Middle Ages. Monks of this age decorated their books with monsters such as the basilisk. This evil creature looked like a cross between a chicken and a serpent!

Many famous monster stories were written in the 19th century, such as *Frankenstein* (1818), *Dracula* (1897) and *The Hunchback of Notre Dame* (1831). Movies are still being made about these monsters. Modern writers such as Stephen King and James Herbert make monsters out of everyday things such as dolls or fog.

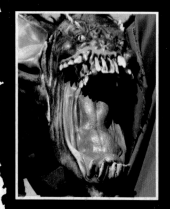

"The cruel monster laughed in his murderous mind, thinking how many people now living would die before the day dawned, how he would stuff his stomach with bloody flesh... he suddenly seized a sleeping soldier, slashed at the flesh, bit through bones and lapped up the blood, greedily feasting on giant lumps. Swiftly he swallowed those lifeless limbs, hands and feet whole."

A description of the swamp monster Grendel from *Beowulf*, written around 1000 AD.

MONSTERS EVERYWHERE

In the 20th century, writers created new robot and alien monsters. In John Wyndham's *The Day of the Triffids* (1951) giant flesh-eating plants invade the Earth. Robots take over the world in Karel Capek's play *Rossum's Universal Robots* (1921).

BEWARE THE TRIFFIDS...they grow ...know...walk...talk...stalk...and KILL!

THE DAY OF THE TRIFFIDS

CINEMASCOPE EASTMAN**COLOR**

HOWARD KEEL
NICOLE MAUREY

MOVIE MONSTERS

It is a calm and sunny day. Suddenly, the sea starts to boil. A ginormous lizard rises up. He thumps onshore, crushing buildings and setting them on fire with his fiery breath. Godzilla is in town.

In early movies such as *Frankenstein* (1931), *The Wolf Man* (1941) and *The Mummy* (1942), most monsters were played by an actor in a costume.

In the 1950s, models were used to create giant monsters on screen. Lots of movies were about Godzilla. This monster lizard is woken by an atomic bomb exploding in the Pacific. In *Them!* (1954) giant ants are created by nuclear tests in the deserts of New Mexico, USA. Thousands flee in terror when the ants start to attack.

Today, computers can create amazing monsters on screen. In *King Kong* (2005) a 7.5-metre gorilla fights equally large dinosaurs. Even when you can't see the monster, movies scare you with loud noises and sudden movements.

THEY CAME FROM OUTER SPACE!

Many movies feature monsters from space. In the 1950s and 60s, "B" movies were made on a small budget. They tried to make scary aliens from bug-eyed turkeys, lobsters and dogs with wigs!

As special effects got better, the monsters became scarier. The *Star Wars* movies are full of weird and wonderful monsters. They come in all shapes, sizes and forms.

NATURAL BORN KILLERS

With an angry screech, T.Rex rushes forward. Jaws open, it crashes into its victim, knocking it over. Huge clawed feet pin down the struggling prey. Razor-sharp teeth tear off giant chunks of flesh.

The *Tyrannosaurus Rex* once roamed all over North America. Luckily for us, it died out 65 million years ago, along with millions of other scary dinosaurs.

A few ancient hunters survive. Crocodiles grow up to 6 metres long. They can kill lions and buffalos. You're also on the menu! Crocodiles wait in shallow waters, then leap out of the water to grab their victim. If their bite doesn't kill you, they'll spin you round and round until you drown.

Deaths and injuries to people from big animals are very rare. Still, there are some scary animals out there. Sharks continue to bite surfers, alligators drag away toddlers, bears maul campers, and tigers attack remote villages.

A DINOSAUR SURVIVOR?

In the swampy jungles of western Africa, many people have reported seeing a strange elephant-sized creature. It has smooth, brownish skin, a long, bendy neck, a very long tail and clawed feet the size of frying pans.

Some scientists believe that this creature, called Mokele-Mbembe by local people, may be a living dinosaur. Since 1980, over 20 expeditions have gone in search of this shy creature, but the beast hasn't turned up – yet!

WHAT ARE MONSTERS?

Good question. Some monsters can be explained as real-life horrors. But what about fire-breathing dragons, giants the size of mountains and other incredible beasts?

In the past, people used myths to explain the world around them. An earthquake was a giant moving under the ground. A whirlpool was a sea monster sucking sailors down. Lightning was two dragons fighting in the sky.

Myths and legends are about real fears. Deadly animal attacks and invading tribes were a constant threat. Warriors wore animal skins to scare their enemies. This is probably where stories about half-human monsters started from.

Modern monsters such as the Yeti may also be real. They are probably not really as scary as we think. The Yeti may just be a large bear or a rare gorilla. Some photographs of monsters are fake, made by people dressed up.

INTO THE UNKNOWN

A few hundred years ago, sailors were afraid of monsters living at the edge of the world. Today, satellites have mapped every part of the planet in great detail. So we worry about them less.

When it comes to outer space, we are not so sure. It's easy to dream up all sorts of strange and terrible aliens! Many look like scary versions of real animals, like spiders, bugs and reptiles.

Coelacanth A large bony fish thought to have died out millions of years ago.

Corpse A dead body.

Crevasse A deep crack in the ice

Demon An evil spirit or monster.

Expedition A journey taken by people who want to find something.

Genes A chemical code passed from parents to their young that contains information such as the colour of our eyes or hair.

Hoax An attempt to trick people into believing that something false is real.

Infect To pass on a disease.

Infra-red Light that is so red we cannot see it. Some cameras use it to make movies in the dark.

Monsters Dangerous, scary creatures.

Mutants Animals or humans whose genes are different. In some stories, mutants have superhuman powers or strength.

Robot An electronic machine that moves like a living person or animal.

Radiation Rays of energy. Can be from a nuclear explosion or chemicals.

Sonar A machine that uses sound to track objects under the water.

Submersibles A small underwater craft used for exploring the deep ocean.

Superhuman Having incredible powers or strength much greater than ordinary humans.

Swarm A large group of things.